IF YOU DON'T
FIGHT
THEN YOU DON'T
WIN

STUDY GUIDE

For foreign and subsidiary rights, contact the author.

Cover design by Sara Young
Cover photo by Andrew van Tilborgh

ISBN: 978-1-960678-61-4   1 2 3 4 5 6 7 8 9 10

Printed in the United States of America

IF YOU DON'T
FIGHT
THEN YOU DON'T
WIN

BECOMING GREAT. ONE BATTLE AT A TIME.

HOPE CARPENTER

STUDY GUIDE

AVAIL

CONTENTS

IF YOU DON'T FIGHT THEN YOU DON'T WIN

BECOMING GREAT. ONE BATTLE AT A TIME.

HOPE CARPENTER

WE WEREN'T PROMISED EASY

I knew that I wanted to fulfill the purpose of God for my life. So, I got up, got on the train, and went for it.

REFLECT AND TAKE ACTION:

Is there an area of your life where you feel like giving up? Where?

_____

_____

_____

_____

_____

_____

Think about a time when you have given up on something important to you. How did this decision impact your life?

_____

_____

_____

_____

_____

_____

Can you identify a situation in the past where you "failed" but chose to persist anyway? What did it teach you about resilience along your spiritual journey?

_____

_____

_____

_____

_____

_____

And we know that in all things, God works
for the good of those who love him, who have
been called according to his purpose..

—Romans 8:28 (NIV)

Consider the scripture above and answer the following questions:

How do you understand the phrase "all things work for good"?

_____

_____

_____

_____

_____

_____

_____

_____

How do you think the apostle Paul would define "good" in the context of this scripture?

_____

_____

_____

_____

_____

_____

_____

_____

_____

Reflect on a time when God turned a failure, disappointment, or personal tragedy into something impactful for the kingdom. How does that experience change the way you think about hardship?

_____

_____

_____

_____

_____

_____

_____

_____

_____

The scripture mentions that all things work for good for those who love God. How do you think love for God influences how we perceive and react to life's challenges?

_____

_____

_____

_____

_____

_____

_____

_____

What can you draw from the story of Joseph in this chapter?

_____

_____

_____

_____

_____

_____

_____

_____

_____

_____

_____

Why do you think getting back up again produces more fruit than aiming for perfection?

_____

_____

_____

_____

_____

_____

_____

_____

_____

_____

_____

_____

In what ways has perfectionism or self-constructed expectations held you back from everything God has for you?

_____

_____

_____

_____

_____

_____

_____

_____

_____

_____

_____

_____

FICKLE FEELINGS

We must take our minds, our thoughts, and meditate (think) the way God does. We must think and say what God says about any given situation—not what we think or feel.

REFLECT AND TAKE ACTION:

What wall have you come up against in your life that seems too difficult to climb or tear down?

_____

_____

_____

_____

_____

_____

_____

_____

_____

What do you think distinguishes someone who doesn't take no for an answer from someone who does? At this point in your life, which category do you most closely identify with?

_____

_____

_____

_____

_____

_____

_____

_____

_____

In what ways do you feel like you allow your feelings to guide you? How does that shape your life?

_____

_____

_____

_____

_____

Why do you think allowing your feelings to dictate your life is dangerous?

_____

_____

_____

_____

_____

All you need to say is simply 'Yes' or 'No'; anything beyond this comes from the evil one.

—Matthew 5:37 (NIV)

Consider the scripture above and answer the following questions:

What does this scripture suggest about the trustworthiness of our emotions?

_____

_____

_____

_____

_____

_____

_____

_____

_____

_____

How does simplicity in our responses to hardship and suffering free us from the prison of our emotional reactions?

_____

_____

_____

_____

_____

_____

_____

_____

What do you think reducing your response to "yes" or "no" looks like practically when you are tempted to believe your emotions?

_____

_____

_____

_____

_____

_____

_____

_____

What did you learn from the stories of Helen Keller, Michael Jordan, and Jamie Kern Lima in this chapter?

_____

_____

_____

_____

_____

_____

_____

_____

_____

_____

How do downward spirals manifest in your life? Describe the process from start to finish.

_____

_____

_____

_____

_____

_____

_____

_____

_____

_____

_____

_____

How can you begin to allow your actions to take over your feelings when you feel like throwing in the towel?

_____

_____

_____

_____

_____

_____

_____

_____

_____

_____

_____

WE HAVE AN ENEMY— BE AWARE

Our lives are the sum of the choices we make.

READING TIME

As you read Chapter 3: "We Have an Enemy—Be Aware" in *If You Don't Fight Then You Don't Win*, reflect on, and respond to the text by answering the following questions.

REFLECT AND TAKE ACTION:

Where in your life do you recognize the enemy at work, trying to derail you or intimidate you from living the life God has for you?

_____

_____

_____

_____

_____

_____

How do you tend to respond to his intimidation tactics?

_____

_____

_____

_____

_____

_____

How have your choices played a role in the enemy's success in beating you out of your goals and purpose when things get hard?

_____

_____

_____

_____

_____

At this, Job got up and tore his robe and shaved his head. Then he fell to the ground in worship and said: "Naked I come from my mother's womb, and naked I will depart. The Lord gave and the Lord has taken away; may the name of the Lord be praised.

—Job 1:20-21 (NIV)

Consider the scripture above and answer the following questions:

What kind of story do you tell yourself about God when something that was important to you is taken away from you?

_____

_____

_____

_____

_____

_____

_____

How do you think your enemy uses this story to wreak havoc on your life? How could you keep that door shut?

_____

_____

_____

_____

_____

_____

_____

_____

Why is God still good and worthy of praise even through loss, devastation, and grief?

_____

_____

_____

_____

_____

_____

What do you think would have happened to Job if he had lost faith? How might the story have ended?

_____

_____

_____

_____

_____

_____

How well do you know the enemy's strategies to wear you out and tear you down? What have you learned about how he tends to sneak into your head?

_____

_____

_____

_____

_____

_____

How could you shift your perspective about your suffering? How do you think the enemy responds to you when you fight back?

_____

_____

_____

_____

_____

_____

_____

_____

_____

_____

Reflect on a time in the past when you have refused the enemy when he came knocking on your door. What was that experience like?

_____

_____

_____

_____

_____

_____

_____

_____

_____

_____

_____

_____

_____

In what ways does God reward His children who press on and take a stand against the enemy?

_____

_____

_____

_____

_____

_____

_____

_____

_____

_____

_____

_____

PRESSURE PRODUCES IF YOU LET IT

Stress and pressure, if not harnessed, can harm us, paralyze us, and ultimately destroy us.

READING TIME

As you read Chapter 4: "Pressure Produces If You Let It" in *If You Don't Fight Then You Don't Win*, reflect on, and respond to the text by answering the following questions.

REFLECT AND TAKE ACTION:

In what ways have you allowed pressure to destroy you rather than shape you and perfect you?

_____

_____

_____

_____

_____

_____

Where are you feeling significant pressure right now in your life? Do you feel harmed by it or sharpened by it?

_____

_____

_____

_____

_____

_____

How does succumbing to the weight of pressure affect your resolve to move closer and closer to God's purpose for your life?

_____

_____

_____

_____

_____

_____

No temptation has overtaken you except what is common to mankind. And God is faithful; he will not let you be tempted beyond what you can bear. But when you are tempted, he will also provide a way out so that you can endure it.

—1 Corinthians 10:13 (NIV)

Consider the scripture above and answer the following questions:

What kind of temptations are you facing right now? Where do you see God's hand amid the temptation?

_____

_____

_____

_____

_____

_____

_____

_____

If there is no temptation uncommon to man, what does that say about whether or not it's worth it to keep fighting?

_____

_____

_____

_____

_____

_____

_____

_____

_____

Describe a time when God offered you a way out of an unbearable temptation. Did you take it? How did everything end?

_____

_____

_____

_____

_____

_____

_____

_____

_____

_____

How could you begin searching for God and expecting Him to make an escape route for you as you navigate through temptation?

_____

_____

_____

_____

_____

_____

_____

_____

_____

_____

Think about where you were one year ago and compare that to where you are now. What role has pressure played in your life over the past year?

_____

_____

_____

_____

_____

_____

_____

_____

In hindsight, do you think pressure has produced something beautiful in you or something invaluable? Why or why not?

_____

_____

_____

_____

_____

_____

_____

_____

What kind of "yucky stuff" (e.g., old hurts, strife, abuse, unforgiveness, hate, judgmentalism, etc.) referenced in this chapter are you holding onto?

_____

_____

_____

_____

_____

_____

_____

_____

_____

How do you think your "yucky stuff" contributes to your responses to pressure?

_____

_____

_____

_____

_____

_____

_____

_____

DIVINELY MOLDED

Listen, if you really want happiness, joy, and fulfillment, if you want to know that you're walking out the purpose and plan of God for your life, don't go "calling looking." Go "God looking."

As you read Chapter 5: "Divinely Molded" in *If You Don't Fight Then You Don't Win*, reflect on, and respond to the text by answering the following questions.

REFLECT AND TAKE ACTION:

Do you feel like you are thriving in life or going through the motions? Why do you think that is?

_____

_____

_____

_____

_____

_____

_____

_____

_____

_____

Do you believe that Jesus will meet you where you are, restore you, reset you, and repurpose you? Why or why not?

_____

_____

_____

_____

_____

_____

_____

_____

_____

_____

When in your life have you taken things into your own hands instead of waiting on God, trusting Him, and allowing Him to do the work that only He can do? How did that turn out?

_____

_____

_____

_____

_____

What does your relationship with God look like these days? Where do you need His grace and help to develop intimacy with Him?

_____

_____

_____

_____

_____

This is the word that came to Jeremiah from the Lord: "Go down to the potter's house, and there I will give you my message." So I went down to the potter's house, and I saw him working at the wheel. But the pot he was shaping from the clay was marred in his hands; so, the potter formed it into another pot, shaping it as seemed best to him.

Then the word of the Lord came to me. He said, "Can I not do with you, Israel, as this potter does?" declares the Lord. "Like clay in the hand of the potter, so are you in my hand, Israel."

—Jeremiah 18:1-6 (NIV)

Consider the scripture above and answer the questions on the following page:

How did Jeremiah respond to God's command to make his way down to the potter's house? How does this response apply to your life right now?

_____

_____

_____

_____

_____

_____

What is your kneejerk reaction to being clay in the Potter's hands? Is it challenging to accept? Encouraging? Describe.

_____

_____

_____

_____

_____

_____

Reflect on "But the pot he was shaping from the clay was marred in his hands." What do you think the author meant by this? What kind of picture does that paint of you and of God?

_____

_____

_____

_____

_____

_____

What do you think would happen if God took you off the potter wheel? What does it look like to stay on the wheel?

_____

_____

_____

_____

_____

_____

In what areas of your life do you have trouble giving up control? Why?

_____

_____

_____

_____

_____

_____

What do you think would happen if you released this area to God? What would He do with it?

_____

_____

_____

_____

_____

_____

What kind of mess in your life, either past or present, feels too big for God to carry and use as an anointing? What do you think is behind that belief?

_____

_____

_____

_____

_____

Is there an area in your life where you struggle to understand what God is doing? What are you tempted to do in order to rectify the uncertainty?

_____

_____

_____

_____

_____

What should you do, and what shouldn't you do in response to uncertainty and confusion?

_____

_____

_____

_____

_____

TROUBLE'S KNOCKING

Here's the thing about battles and trouble.... You really don't know what's in you until it's tested.

READING TIME

As you read Chapter 6: "Trouble's Knocking" in *If You Don't Fight Then You Don't Win*, reflect on, and respond to the text by answering the following questions.

REFLECT AND TAKE ACTION:

What kind of unexpected surprises have you encountered in your life, and how did they throw you for a loop? What did you expect and why?

_____
_____
_____
_____
_____

In what ways has your "conditioning" for war (through trouble and hardship) equipped you for other wars that you have or will face in your lifetime?

_____
_____
_____
_____
_____

When was the last time unanticipated trouble paid you a visit? How did you respond? What could you do to respond in a way that upholds the truths of the Bible?

_____
_____
_____
_____
_____

How does it feel to know that other battles are coming down the road? How can you begin preparing for them?

_____

_____

_____

_____

_____

_____

When you pass through the waters, I will be with you; and when you pass through the rivers, they will not sweep over you. When you walk through the fire, you will not be burned; the flames will not set you ablaze.

—Isaiah 43:2 (NIV)

Consider the scripture above and answer the following questions:

In what ways have you felt God's presence with you when you have walked through the fiery furnace of life?

_____

_____

_____

_____

_____

_____

What do the images of water and fire symbolize in your life?

_____

_____

_____

_____

_____

_____

_____

_____

Can you recall a time when you felt overwhelmed yet found strength or a way out that you didn't expect?

_____

_____

_____

_____

_____

_____

_____

When you are wading through deep waters and walking through fire, what does His protection look like? What does it not look like?

_____

_____

_____

_____

_____

_____

_____

_____

How do you think God has taken your choices and past into consideration when He designed your future? In what ways does this offer you comfort?

_____

_____

_____

_____

_____

_____

If God goes before us and fights our battles, what should we be doing in the meantime? How do we partner with God and allow Him to do the heavy lifting at the same time?

_____

_____

_____

_____

_____

_____

What kind of life are you striving to live? What does the "good life" look like to you? Explain.

_____

_____

_____

_____

_____

_____

What is consuming your heart and mind these days? Where is Jesus in the middle of all of it?

_____

_____

_____

_____

_____

_____

How does the object of our focus pull us farther away from God or nearer to Him? Where do you fall on that continuum right now?

_____

_____

_____

_____

_____

How can we use trouble as a resource for—not a hindrance to—finishing the race and finishing it well?

_____

_____

_____

_____

_____

_____

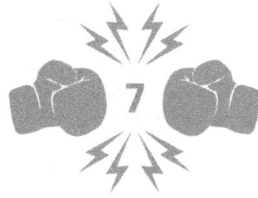

HOW'S YOUR HEART?

IT IS IMPERATIVE that we stop, step off the track of life, lie on the operating table, allow the Lord to examine our hearts, and then rid them of the pain we've been carrying so that we can heal and gain our strength to be ready to run again.

As you read Chapter 7: "How's Your Heart?" in *If You Don't Fight Then You Don't Win*, reflect on, and respond to the text by answering the following questions.

REFLECT AND TAKE ACTION:

What kind of bitterness, resentment, anger, or hurt are you currently harboring?

_____

_____

_____

_____

_____

_____

What root has taken up residence in the soil of your heart, and what kind of fruit is it producing?

_____

_____

_____

_____

_____

_____

Envision the place and person you aspire to be. What does your heart look like, and how does it compare with the condition of your heart now?

_____

_____

_____

_____

_____

_____

In what ways does the source of bad soil (e.g., fractured relationships, sin, illness) weaken our resolve to fight through turmoil in our lives?

_____

_____

_____

_____

_____

_____

For the joy set before him, he endured the cross, scorning its shame, and sat down at the right hand of the throne of God.

—Hebrews 12:2 (NIV)

Consider the scripture above and answer the following questions:

How do you think Jesus endured such great suffering on the cross while also keeping His heart pure, clean, and free of sin at the same time? How can those two grow together?

_____

_____

_____

_____

_____

_____

_____

_____

_____

What joy is set before you? What cross are you bearing right now, and why is sticking it out worth it?

_____

_____

_____

_____

_____

_____

_____

_____

_____

_____

How did Jesus's trouble compare to the glory of His position alongside the Father now? What can you glean from this as it relates to your troubles?

_____

_____

_____

_____

_____

_____

_____

_____

_____

_____

What role do transparency and vulnerability play in cultivating the heart we need to persevere and win?

_____

_____

_____

_____

_____

_____

_____

_____

What pain, heartache, or sin have you yet to air out, confess, and address? Where could you begin?

_____

_____

_____

_____

_____

_____

_____

_____

What will happen if you make a home in the handicaps, misery, and grief of your past? What will happen if you step out in faith and deal with them head-on?

_____

_____

_____

_____

_____

_____

_____

_____

What kind of steps could you take today toward forgiving someone who has betrayed you or crossed you?

_____

_____

_____

_____

_____

_____

_____

FIGHT THE GOOD FIGHT OF FAITH

The prescription for every trial is the Word of God, and you must know the Word of God. God's Word is your weapon against the enemy.

As you read Chapter 8: "Fight the Good Fight of Faith" in *If You Don't Fight Then You Don't Win*, reflect on, and respond to the text by answering the following questions.

REFLECT AND TAKE ACTION:

In what ways do you feel like you are waiting for greatness and God's eternal purpose for you to find you? How do you think waiting will serve this purpose?

_____

_____

_____

_____

_____

_____

_____

_____

What would it look like to fight for God's purpose for your life instead of waiting for it?

_____

_____

_____

_____

_____

_____

_____

_____

_____

_____

What are some things about your walk with God and experience with Christianity that have surprised you? Why?

_____

_____

_____

_____

_____

_____

How would you describe "work" as it relates to holding fast to faith and remaining uncompromising about the Word of God?

_____

_____

_____

_____

_____

_____

What is your greatest weapon in fighting for your faith when the enemy comes to whisper in your ear? How often do you wield it?

_____

_____

_____

_____

_____

_____

> And this small and temporary trouble we suffer will bring us a tremendous and eternal glory, much greater than the trouble. For we fix our attention, not on things that are seen, but on things that are unseen. What can be seen lasts only for a time, but what cannot be seen lasts forever.
>
> —2 Corinthians 4:17-18 (GNT)

Consider the scripture above and answer the questions on the following page:

Why is what we see a poor litmus test for what is possible and what is to come? In what ways are you limiting yourself by relying on what you see in the natural?

_____

_____

_____

_____

_____

_____

_____

How does thinking about the permanence of eternal glory change the way you see your troubles here on earth?

_____

_____

_____

_____

_____

_____

_____

How might your present troubles work towards those things that are long-lasting, productive, and fulfilling?

_____

_____

_____

_____

_____

_____

_____

_____

How well do you know the Word? How deeply is it written on your heart?

_____

_____

_____

_____

_____

_____

_____

_____

Is your faith a witness to the glorious things God can do with your troubles, or is it a testament to defeat and self-pity? Explain your answer.

_____

_____

_____

_____

_____

_____

_____

_____

Have you ever experienced the freedom of being unencumbered by something that should be encumbering? How was God intervening to lift the burden of those heavy things?

_____

_____

_____

_____

_____

_____

_____

_____

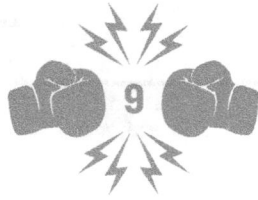

WHAT'S STOPPING YOU?

*If we will trust God with the little
that we have, God will turn it
into something powerful.*

READING TIME

As you read Chapter 9: "What's Stopping You?" in *If You Don't Fight Then You Don't Win*, reflect on, and respond to the text by answering the following questions.

REFLECT AND TAKE ACTION:

What do you feel you are unqualified for in your life right now or in the past?

_____
_____
_____
_____
_____
_____
_____
_____
_____

Why are your qualifications or lack thereof of no interest or consequence to God? What would happen if every decision you made was based on whether you felt qualified?

_____
_____
_____
_____
_____
_____
_____
_____
_____
_____

Recall a time when God took something small and made it abundant. How did that impact your faith and drive it away from mediocrity?

_____

_____

_____

_____

_____

_____

_____

_____

_____

_____

Why do you think God's plan for your life has to reach beyond your abilities?

_____

_____

_____

_____

_____

_____

_____

_____

_____

_____

My grace is all you need. My power works
best in weakness. So now I am glad to boast
about my weaknesses, so that the power
of Christ can work through me.

—1 Corinthians 12:9 (NLT)

Consider the scripture above and answer the following questions:

In what areas of your life might your weaknesses be an asset
for the kingdom of God?

_____

_____

_____

_____

_____

_____

_____

_____

When have you seen God's power at its greatest in your life?
Where were you, what were you doing, and how did you feel?

_____

_____

_____

_____

_____

_____

_____

_____

If you were to boast about your weaknesses, what would they be, and what might you say?

_____

_____

_____

_____

_____

_____

_____

_____

What is an area of weakness in your life that God is using to reinvent you and declare His glory and power over your own? Why do you think He is working on that?

_____

_____

_____

_____

_____

_____

_____

_____

What prayers have you been waiting for God to answer that have not yet been fulfilled?

_____

_____

_____

_____

_____

_____

_____

_____

How might discrepancies between your desired timing and His timing create fertile ground for being tempted to give up?

_____

_____

_____

_____

_____

_____

_____

_____

WE WIN

Our lives will be built day by day, month by month, year by year, failure by failure, and victory by victory.

READING TIME

As you read Chapter 10: "We Win" in *If You Don't Fight Then You Don't Win*, reflect on, and respond to the text by answering the following questions.

REFLECT AND TAKE ACTION:

Have you ever come close to giving up in a valley that felt insurmountable? Why did you or didn't you?

_____

_____

_____

_____

_____

_____

Why do you think it's so easy to forget the mountains and instead be consumed by the valleys?

_____

_____

_____

_____

_____

_____

What does relying on the truth of God's Word over facts look like practically? Use an experience in your own life as an example, and describe it.

_____

_____

_____

_____

_____

_____

In what ways do vigilance and sober-mindedness guard us against the temptation to give up?

_____

_____

_____

_____

_____

_____

_____

_____

_____

_____

How is your life now evidence of your ability to push past the seasons that have chewed you up and spit you out?

_____

_____

_____

_____

_____

_____

_____

_____

_____

_____

_____

But let us who are of the day be sober,
putting on the breastplate of faith and love,
and as a helmet the hope of salvation.

—1 Thessalonians 5:8 (NKJV)

Consider the scripture above and answer the following questions:

In your own words, what does it mean to be "sober"? How well do you remain sober in times of trouble?

_____

_____

_____

_____

_____

_____

_____

_____

How does the imagery of acting like a soldier with armor lend itself to relentless perseverance?

_____

_____

_____

_____

_____

_____

_____

_____

What do you think having the hope of salvation as a helmet does for keeping your eyes on the prize and not giving in to pressure?

_____

_____

_____

_____

_____

_____

_____

_____

_____

Can you detect a counterfeit from what's real? Why or why not?

_____

_____

_____

_____

_____

_____

_____

_____

Think of a time when you took the bait of a counterfeit narrative that said you'd never make it through. If you could teleport yourself back to that time, what would you tell yourself?

_____

_____

_____

_____

_____

_____

_____

In what ways have you seen God's unwavering faithfulness in your life? List five occasions when He rescued you or saw you through an impossible situation.

_____

_____

_____

_____

_____

_____

_____